PORTSMOUTH'S TRAMWAYS

Series editor Robert J Harley

Martin Petch

MP Middleton Press

Cover Picture: A wonderfully animated Edwardian scene is revealed at Clarence Pier, possibly on the 1903 August bank holiday. Note the two ex-horsecars 82 and 83 as well as 37. (W.Gunnell/J.C.Bell Coll.).

Cover Colours: These depict the livery of scarlet and white introduced by Portsmouth Corporation in 1930.

**Dedicated to Eric Dash, 1920 - 1994,
a Portsmouth man who affectionately
recalled the old trams, and lobbied
tirelessly for modern Light Rail
in Hampshire.**

First published March 1996

ISBN 1 873793 72 3

© Middleton Press 1996

Design - Deborah Goodridge

*Published by Middleton Press
           Easebourne Lane
           Midhurst
           West Sussex
           GU29 9AZ
           Tel: 01730 813169
           Fax: 01730 812601*

*Printed & bound by Biddles Ltd,
          Guildford and Kings Lynn*

CONTENTS

Guildhall - Clarence Pier	1
Guildhall - Floating Bridge	10
Guildhall - Dockyard	16
Dockyard - East Southsea	21
Southsea - Eastney - Milton	33
Guildhall - Copnor	56
Landport - Twyford Avenue	65
Fratton Bridge - Cosham	73
Finale	95
Horse Cars	100
Lifu	104
Electric Cars	105

INTRODUCTION AND ACKNOWLEDGEMENTS

When I started gathering material for this book, most of the photographs were close-up views of trams at similar locations - Cosham, Guildhall, and so on. There are two people I must thank above all for enabling me to present this much wider selection of scenes which now covers most of the streets once served by tramway, and over a wider time-span. The first is George Tucker, who carefully photographed many locations, often just before the change to trolleybuses; second is Tom Dethridge who kindly made available to me his large collection lovingly gathered over several decades.

S E Harrison's classic book *The Tramways of Portsmouth* forms the basis of the text, together with Leslie Bern's researches. My thanks go to Mr Bern as well as to Barry Cox and Stephen Pomeroy for helping me to fill the last few gaps in the story; also to Stephen and Lorraine Low for the use of their PC. I am indebted to Terry Russell who produced most of the car plans.

The Ordnance Survey County Series map extracts, from the 1910 or 1933 editions, were supplied by Portsmouth City and Hampshire County Record Offices. Mr John Gillham has kindly permitted me to use two of his track plans, and Godfrey Croughton has supplied the tickets.

I have arranged the chapters of this book by area, so that the character of Portsmouth's suburbs can be appreciated. The Provincial Tramways, Gosport - Fareham and the Portsdown and Horndean Light Railway, will form a separate volume.

GEOGRAPHICAL SETTING

Portsea Island is part of a low-lying area of south-east Hampshire indented by numerous creeks and inlets: to the west is Gosport, whilst Hayling Island lies to the east. Portsdown Hill forms a natural barrier along the north side. Portsmouth Harbour is an ideal site for a naval base, and over the years the urban development has spread beyond the confines of the island, now virtually linking up to Fareham and Havant.

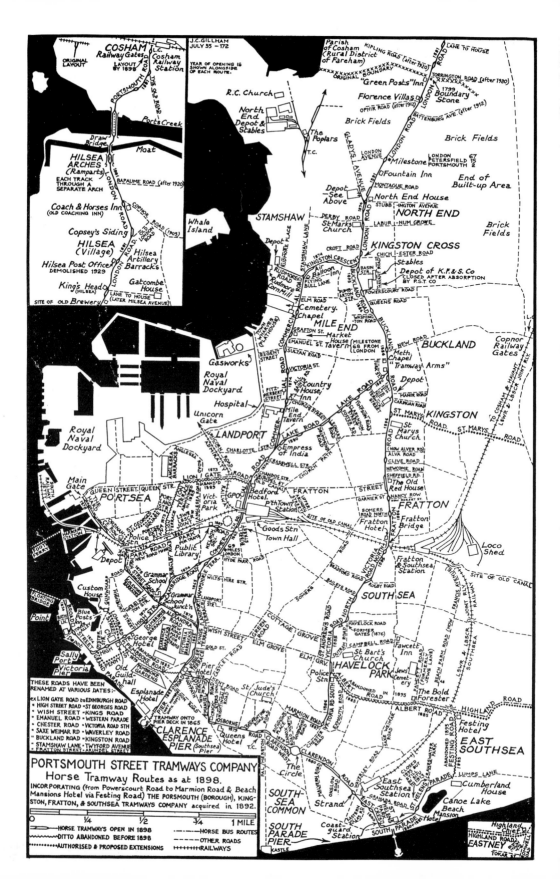

PORTSMOUTH STREET TRAMWAYS COMPANY
Horse Tramway Routes as at 1898.

INCORPORATING (from Powerscourt Road to Marmion Road & Beach Mansions Hotel via Festing Road) THE PORSMOUTH (BOROUGH), KINGSTON, FRATTON, & SOUTHSEA TRAMWAYS COMPANY acquired in 1892.

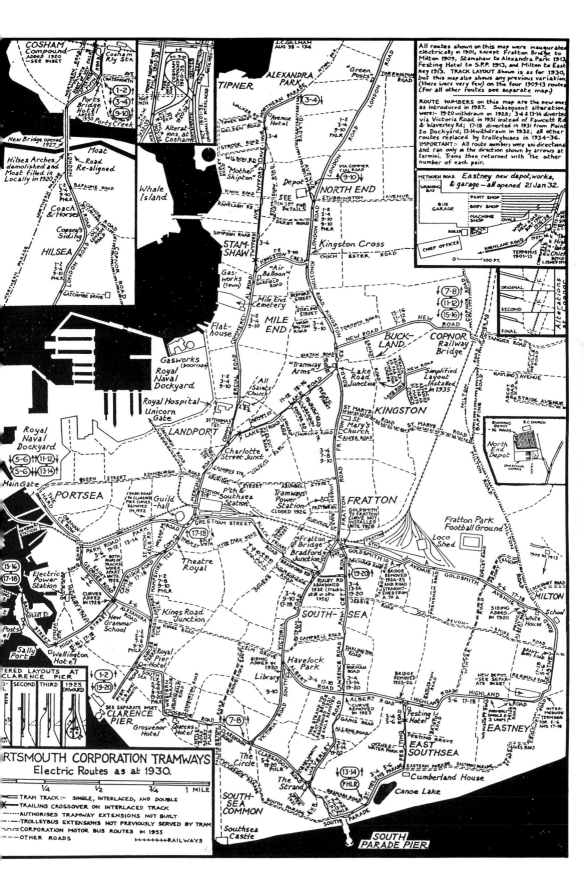

PORTSMOUTH CORPORATION TRAMWAYS
Electric Routes as at 1930.

¼	½	¾	1 MILE	

— TRAM TRACK:— SINGLE, INTERLACED, AND DOUBLE
✕ — TRAILING CROSSOVER ON INTERLACED TRACK
········ AUTHORISED TRAMWAY EXTENSIONS NOT BUILT
—·—·— TROLLEYBUS EXTENSIONS NOT PREVIOUSLY SERVED BY TRAM
═══ CORPORATION MOTOR BUS ROUTES IN 1955
— OTHER ROADS
+++++++RAILWAYS

J.C.GILLHAM
AUG 55 – 174

All routes shown on this map were inaugurated electrically in 1901, except Fratton Bridge to Milton 1909, Stamshaw to Alexandra Park 1913, Festing Hotel to S.P.P. 1913, and Milton to East ney 1913. TRACK LAYOUT shown is as for 1930, but this map also shows any previous variation (there were very few) on the four 1909-13 routes. (For all other routes see separate map.)

ROUTE NUMBERS on this map are the new ones as introduced in 1927. Subsequent alterations were:— 19-20 withdrawn in 1928; 3-4 & 13-14 diverted via Victoria Road in 1931 instead of Fawcett Rd & Waverley Rd; 17-18 diverted in 1931 from Point to Dockyard; 13-14 withdrawn in 1932; all other routes replaced by trolleybuses in 1934-36. IMPORTANT:— All route numbers were uni-directional and ran only in the direction shown by arrows at termini. Trams then returned with the other number of each pair.

METHUEN ROAD. Eastney new depot, works, & garage—all opened 21 Jan 32.

COSHAM
Compound
Added 1920
—SEE INSET

HISTORICAL BACKGROUND

Portsmouth's association with the Navy stretches back through many royal connections as far as King Alfred the Great. Much of the local industry has traditionally been defence-related and the people are justifiably proud of this association. The heroism of generations of seafarers is commemorated by many monuments and museums, not least within the Dockyard itself.

Within and around the Dockyard's fortifications there developed communities, notably Landport and Portsea. These densely populated areas produced such notables as I K Brunel and Charles Dickens. There was much poverty; this was relieved in spirit both by High Church Anglicanism and by the numerous alehouses by which one still navigates round the city. In contrast, Southsea developed during the last century as a more genteel district, and as a seaside resort.

Into this colourful world came a very early tramway proposal: the Landport & Southsea Tramways Company obtained an Act of Parliament in 1863 for a line linking the Town Station (Portsmouth & Southsea) with Clarence Pier. This was for the onward conveyance of passengers and freight to the Isle of Wight; the Harbour Station did not open until 1876. Trams started running on 15th May 1865; they used an unusual track gauge of 4ft. 7 ¾ins./1416mm. This was adopted to enable standard gauge (4ft. 8½ins./1435mm) railway wagons and vans to be hauled through the streets. The discrepancy in gauge is accounted for by the fact that the distance between the tramway rails was tailored to fit the flanges of the wider railway wheels.

In 1872, the Provincial Tramways Co Ltd was registered, together with subsidiary companies to operate lines in Cardiff, Plymouth and Portsmouth. Their line from Broad Street to North End opened in 1874. Meanwhile the General Tramway Company of Portsmouth Ltd promoted a line linking South Parade Pier with The Hard and with Broad Street. In 1878 Provincial took control of the other companies and continued expansion, reaching Cosham in 1881. It reached its maximum size in 1893, with 14 route miles, 58 trams and 249 horses.

Portsmouth Corporation should have taken over at midnight, 31st December 1899, but protracted legal wrangling delayed this for a year. Provincial had plans of their own for a line to Horndean, and wanted more than the scrap value of their assets. The final settlement gave the Corporation running rights to Portsdown Hill.

During 1901 the Corporation undertook a remarkably vigorous conversion programme, rebuilding the entire network: 23½ miles/38kms of track had been laid in eight months! North End depot was rebuilt and a new power station inaugurated in Vivash Road, Fratton, to cope with the 80 electric trams on order. On 24th September 1901 the line from North End to Clarence Pier was re-opened; the last horse trams ran in May 1903.

Mr Spaven who managed the undertaking for 24 years from 1902, introduced an all-over 10-minute service with interchange points. Route letters were displayed from 1914. Important track extensions were Goldsmith Avenue in 1909 followed in 1913 by Twyford Avenue, Festing Road and Eastney Road. A 1903 proposal to link Eastney with Hayling Island via a bridge never proceeded.

After the deprivations of the 1914-1918 war, 12 covered-top cars were bought in 1920. Portsmouth became a city on 21st April 1926, at which time the dynamic Ben Hall took charge. He started car overhauls and rebuilds, continued track improvements and had the new number 1 built in 1930.

Attention turned to the trolleybus at this time, and the first ones ran in 1934. Originally it was intended to run them alongside trams for several years, but subsequently a total conversion plan was implemented. The last tram ran on 10th November 1936. The trolleybuses in turn gave way to diesel buses on 27th July 1963, and in today's de-regulated climate Portsmouth is served by a plethora of minibuses.

TRAM ROUTES IN 1927:

1 (ex A) - Cosham-Kingston Cres-Guildhall-
    Clarence Pier.
2 (ex A) - Reverse of 1.
3 (ex X) - Cosham-Fawcett Rd-South Parade Pier
    (SPP)-Albert Rd-Guildhall-Twyford Av.
4 (ex B) - Reverse of 3.
5 (ex C) - Dockyard-Osborne Rd-SPP-Eastney-Milton-
    Guildhall-Dockyard.
6 (ex C) - Reverse of 5.
7 (ex D) - Copnor-Fratton Bridge-Guildhall-
    Palmerston Rd or Clarence Pier.
8 (ex D) - Reverse of 7.
9 (ex O) - Cosham-Fratton Rd-Victoria Rd-Osborne
    Rd-Guildhall-Kingston Cres-North End.

10 (ex O) - Reverse of 9.
11 (ex F) - Copnor-Lake Rd-Dockyard.
12 (ex F) - Reverse of 11.
13 (ex G) - Dockyard-Guildhall-Fawcett Rd-SPP.
14 (ex G) - Reverse of 13.
15 (ex J) - Copnor-Lake Rd-Floating Bridge.
16 (ex J) - Reverse of 15.
17 (ex L) - Floating Bridge-Guildhall-Albert Rd-
        Eastney-Milton-Fratton Bridge-Guildhall.
18 (ex Z) - Reverse of 17.
19 (ex T) - Fratton Bridge-Fawcett Rd-
        Strand-Clarence Pier.
20 (ex T) - Reverse of 19.
PHLR- Portsdown and Horndean Light Railway trams
operating from Horndean to South Parade Pier.

It is interesting to note the use of different numbers depending on the direction of travel. Routes changed considerably over the years, and the above is only a snapshot.

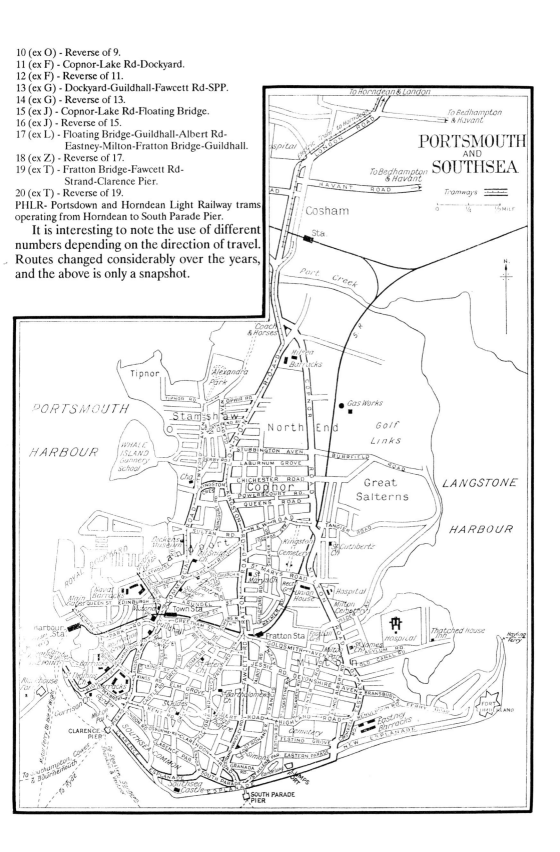

1. Our travels start at the system's hub - outside Portsmouth Guildhall. Built as the Town Hall in 1890, this imposing structure was gutted in the Blitz of 1941, but survives minus its cupola. (J.Welch & Sons/T.Dethridge Coll.)

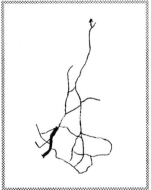

2. The horse tramway of 1865 would have entered the Town Station where the wagon is seen; this is 1901 and the new electric car is on driver-training duties. Note the absence of destination indicators. Passengers on a passing horsecar look on in anticipation. (B.Cox Coll.)

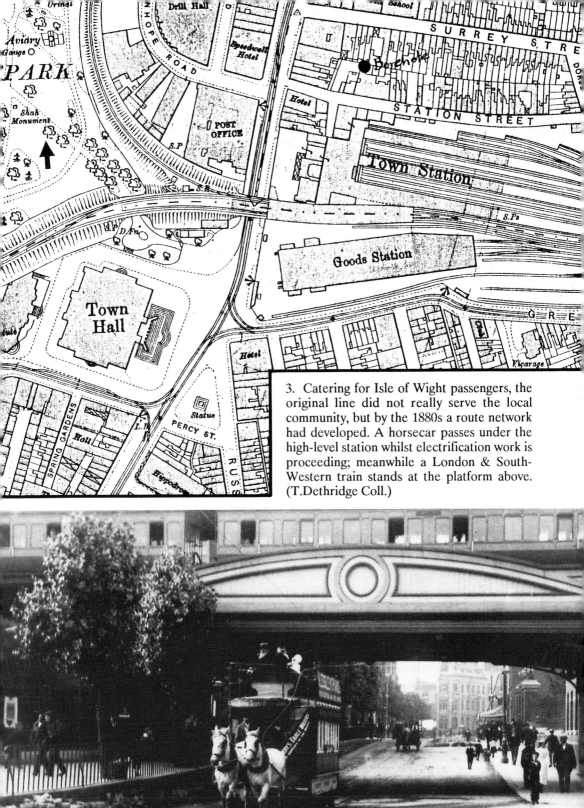

3. Catering for Isle of Wight passengers, the original line did not really serve the local community, but by the 1880s a route network had developed. A horsecar passes under the high-level station whilst electrification work is proceeding; meanwhile a London & South-Western train stands at the platform above. (T.Dethridge Coll.)

←

4. Buswells Corner is the junction of Kings Road and Landport Terrace; the tram on the left is going to Beach Mansions (South Parade Pier) while number 63 is heading for the Dockyard. (T.Dethridge Coll.)

6. Under a leaden sky, Southsea Common has flooded, possibly in March of 1913. In the background are the imposing Victoria Barracks. (S.Cribb/T.Dethridge Coll.)

←

5. Moving south, tram 93 passes Kings Terrace - it is about to turn left into Alexandra Road (today Museum Road). Only the central part of this building survives.
(G.A.Tucker/T.Dethridge Coll.)

7. The track in Pier Road was originally laid on the east side; this tram has just arrived from Cosham. (T.Dethridge Coll.)

8. In order to connect with the ferries, the 1865 line went right on to Clarence Pier where there was a platform. This is one of the original cars with its primitive iron stair and back-to-back knifeboard seat on top. Note also the flat wagon for goods traffic.
(Portsmouth City Record Office)

9. In 1925 a turning loop was added to the congested stub terminus; enclosed car 116 is a far cry from the spartan days of horse traction!
(M.J.OConnor/J.C.Bell Coll.)

GUILDHALL - FLOATING BRIDGE

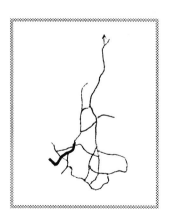

10. Returning now to the city centre, we board another tram for the trip to the Floating Bridge. Car 90 was one of the second batch of new trams with direct stairs.
(M.J.OConnor/T.Dethridge Coll.)

11. A little way down Commercial Road (now Guildhall Walk) car 62 is passing the Theatre Royal - note the early revolving indicator box and the reversed stairs of the first 80 trams. These elegant buildings happily survive, including a wall-rosette on the Prudential office. (W.H.Smith/T.Dethridge Coll.)

12. In the High Street the old Guildhall with its Classical front can be seen behind the tram. Many of these buildings perished in the Blitz and on the left the Cathedral is now fully visible. In spite of this upheaval you can still sense a link with the past. (L.Levy/T.Dethridge Coll.)

13. Looking north along Broad Street car 51 passes the Seagull pub on 11th April 1936. Further on to the right is the depot where various vehicles were being restored in 1996, including Horndean cars 5 and 13. (G.A.Tucker/T.Dethridge Coll.)

14. Not exactly an integrated transport system, but an exceptional tide flooding Broad Street! Car 39 prepares to wade off to Eastney. On the right is the floating bridge's chain windlass. (T.Dethridge Coll.)

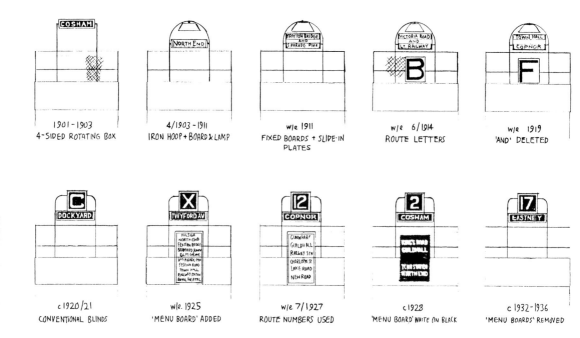

1901-1903 4-SIDED ROTATING BOX	4/1903-1911 IRON HOOP + BOARD & LAMP	w/e 1911 FIXED BOARDS + SLIDE-IN PLATES	w/e 6/1914 ROUTE LETTERS	w/e 1919 'AND' DELETED

c1920/21 CONVENTIONAL BLINDS	w/e 1925 'MENU BOARD' ADDED	w/e 7/1927 ROUTE NUMBERS USED	c1928 'MENU BOARD' WHITE ON BLACK	c1932-1936 'MENU BOARDS' REMOVED

15. The same terminus, looking north. In the distance is a battleship and three paddle steamers; the carts are queuing for the Gosport floating bridge. Stories of trams running off into the water here have been told - they certainly reached the shingle once or twice! The later track layout - a passing loop and single stub - can still be seen today. (R.J.Harley Coll.)

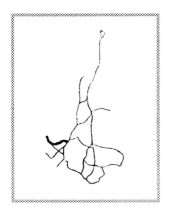

16. Back again to Guildhall Square - or rather Park Road. Two ex-horse trams await the rush-hour. Behind is the College of Science and Technology, later to become part of the new University of Portsmouth. (O.J.Morris)

17. Moving a little further along Park Road, trams 3 and 44 cross in May 1936 - their Indian summer. Sadly, Butterfield's fine church of St. Michael and All Angels was pulled down in 1960. By a cruel irony the whole street is now blocked by the University's monolithic School of Architecture Building!
(G.A.Tucker/T.Dethridge Coll.)

18. An Edwardian view of the Hard is depicted here with the Dockyard gate behind. Today HMS Warrior is moored to the left; HMS Victory was dry-docked in 1922. If the County's plans are realised the Fareham light rail line may one day pass under here.
(T.Dethridge Coll.)

19. Two trams stand at the Hard - the car on the right is carrying the new livery of scarlet rather than crimson lake. (A.D.Packer Coll.)

20. Standing outside the Keppels Head Hotel, Mr Priestley took this view of the Hard on 4th August 1936. The trolleybus wires are about to be strung; a train is in the Harbour station. (H.B.Priestley/T.Dethridge Coll.)

DOCKYARD - EAST
SOUTHSEA

21. Our tour continues by returning from the Dockyard towards Southsea. Now in her dry dock, the Victory's masts are visible. Car 8 is looking rather shabby, and the apron (as the dash was known in Portsmouth) has been patched. (J.C.Bell Coll.)

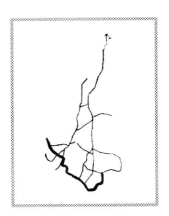

22. On 10th March 1935 smart number 105 is passing the Grammar School. High Street is to the left and St Georges Road is behind the tram. This crossing was known to crews as Cambridge Junction, or "Clapham Junction" in honour of the frequent tram service! (G.A.Tucker/T.Dethridge Coll.)

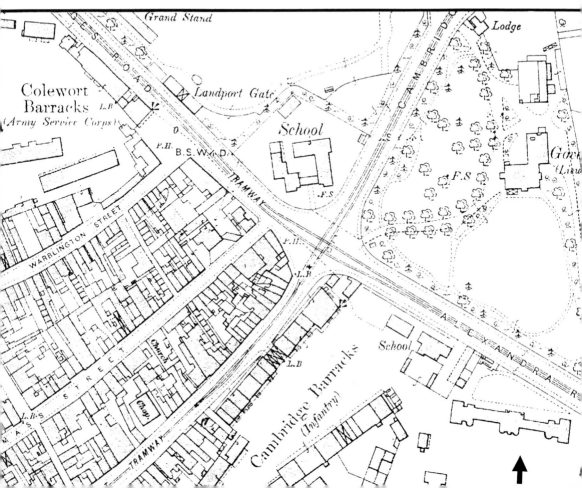

23. Returning to Buswells Corner in an earlier age, a two-horse tram heads from Alexandra Road into Kings Terrace. The buildings visible in Landport Terrace are still standing. (T.Dethridge Coll.)

24. Outside the recently-demolished Royal Pier Hotel was the junction with Southsea Terrace, recorded in October 1936. (G.A.Tucker/T.Dethridge Coll.)

25. The residents of Osborne Road opposed the original horse tramway - here we see one of many examples of interlaced track by the Queens Hotel. Car 67 is on the loop by Ashburton Road. Is the elegant lady in the window (left) looking at the photographer or waiting for the milkman?
(J.Valentine/T.Dethridge Coll.)

26. Handleys store was on the corner of Osborne Road and Palmerston Road. A cor-poration-owned horsecar trundles past with sunblinds in place. While the district generally retains its Victorian, holiday appeal, this junction was destroyed by enemy action in the Second World War. (T.Dethridge Coll.)

27. Beyond The Circle, Clarendon Road
meanders on past many fine Southsea villas. In
March 1933 a Horndean bound Light Railway
car runs wrong-line during track relaying work.
(G.A.Tucker/T.Dethridge Coll.)

South Parade Pier, Southsea.

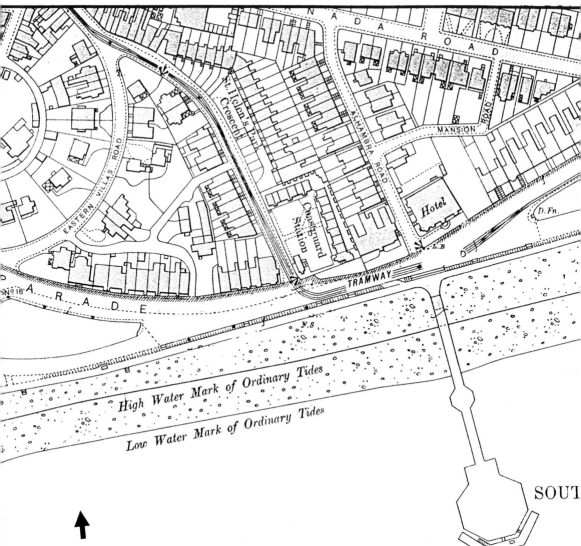

CANADA ROAD

St. Helen's Parade

Crescent

EASTERN VILLAS ROAD

MANSION ROAD

ALHAMBRA ROAD

Hotel

D. Fn.

Coastguard Station

L.B.

TRAMWAY

No. 18 PARADE

F.S.

High Water Mark of Ordinary Tides

Low Water Mark of Ordinary Tides

SOUT

Landing Stag

28. Having traversed Southsea inland, the tramway emerged on to South Parade, passing the Edwardian pier where a third track was provided. (Miltons/J.C.Bell Coll.)

29. At the same spot as the previous view, car 111 awaits its return to the Dockyard by the Beach Mansions Hotel. Today minibuses swarm around this roadway. (T.Dethridge Coll.)

30. In order to stave off bus competition, the PHLR cars regularly ran through into Portsmouth after April 1927, terminating at South Parade Pier. The conductor of car 10 is walking the trolley pole round. (G.A.Tucker/T.Dethridge Coll.)

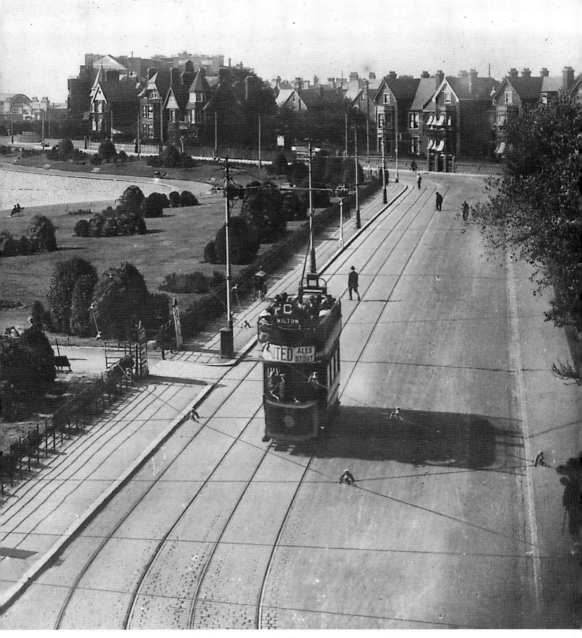

31. Continuing eastwards, the tramway passed
along St. Helens Parade. Today both the Pier
and the Canoe Lake are as popular as ever.
(J.C.Bell Coll.)

32. Any route extension was ceremonially
inaugurated - on 31st July 1913 the dignitaries
feting the Festing Road extension are seen
here posing for posterity on the corner of
Eastern Parade. This link enabled the new B/X
circular service to operate from Cosham to
Twyford Avenue. (T.Dethridge Coll.)

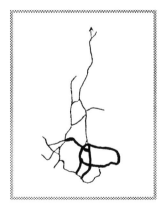

33. Proceeding up Victoria Road South from The Circle, we encounter car 44 at the Marmion Road stop. The original horse tramway turned into this road to serve the shopping area. (O.J.Morris/B.Cox Coll.)

34. Victoria Road North passes through an area consisting of large villas - today it is bedsit land. This is the curve by Outram Road. (S.E.Harrison/B.Cox Coll.)

35. Although no track turned right at Bradford Junction, we now cut along Rugby Road, where the tramlines survive to this day - a fine example of the interlaced track so favoured in Portsmouth. (M.Petch)

36. Car 43 has just crossed the junction with Rugby Road (left) on its way down Fawcett Road in March 1931. Mr. Tucker thoughtfully recorded this scene just in time.
(G.A.Tucker/T.Dethridge Coll.)

37. Further down, Fawcett Road bears left by the Fawcett Inn; car 28 is entering the interlaced track in Lawrence Road, again on 14th March 1931. This stretch of line closed on 19th April 1931 and the rails were immediately lifted. The 3/4 service was diverted to Victoria Road.
(G.A.Tucker/T.Dethridge Coll.)

Albert Road, Southsea. 42.

38. Lawrence Road meets Albert Road and continues as Waverley Road (previously Saxe-Weimar Road). This view shows 91 heading west in Albert Road; a circular service car is crossing southbound. (T.Dethidge Coll.)

39. Immediately after the junction with Victoria Road we encounter the imposing Kings Theatre, opened in 1907. The Albert Road shopping area remains largely unchanged in appearance.
(J.Welch & Sons/T.Dethridge Coll.)

40. Car 15 passes the Trinity Methodist Church by Francis Avenue - the stylish brick campanile is out of view. Beyond is the ramp over the Southsea Railway which the trams had seen off in 1914, five years before this view.
(J.C.Bell Coll.)

N 4572
Portsmouth Corporation Trys.

Service Nos. 3 & 4		
3	**3**d	9
4		10
5		11
6		12
		13
8		14
9		15
10		16
11		17

Issued subject to the Corporation Bye-laws and available only on Car which issued & to Station opposite punch hole. Must be shown for Inspection or given up on demand.

Punch & Ticket Co., London M

A 24764
Portsmouth Corporation Trys.

Cosham	**1**d	P.O. Hilsea
Copsey's		North End
North End		All Saints
Twyford Avenue		Town Hall
All Saints		King's Road
Town Hall		Clarence Pier

Issued subject to the Corporation Bye-laws and available only on Car on which issued, and to the Station opposite punch hole. Must be shown for Inspection or given up on demand.

Punch & Ticket Co., Ltd., London

41. Highland Road, Eastney, just beyond Festing Road, seen in seemingly far-off Edwardian days. No doubt the people were urged to keep still by the local photographer! Can anyone recognise themselves?
(Barkshire Bros/T.Dethridge Coll.)

42. Until 1936 the trams had fixed-head trolley wheels, the overhead wire being aligned above the track - but in order to use the positive trolleybus wire, swivel-heads were fitted for the transition period. Passing Highland Road cemetery in October 1936, car 51s pole barely reaches the new wires.
(G.A.Tucker/T.Dethridge Coll.)

43. On 21st January 1932 a new depot, garage and offices were opened at Eastney, opposite the site of the Highland Chief. This pub had been removed in 1916 to iron out a blind corner. Also at this point, the proposed Hayling Island route would have continued along Henderson Road. Today this site is occupied by housing, but the offices survive as Southsea Police Station.
(G.A.Tucker/T.Dethridge Coll.)

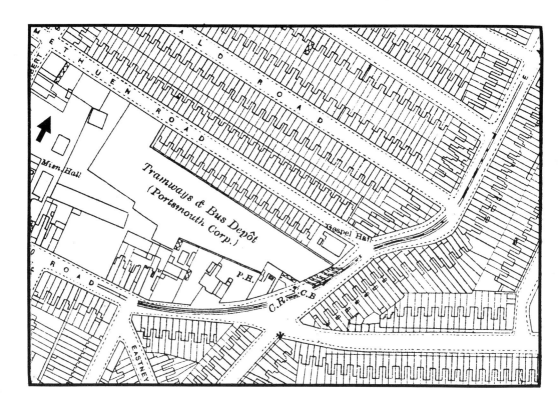

44. The afternoon shift turns out at Eastney in
1934/5. (T.Dethridge Coll.)

45. The link-up between the Highland Chief, Eastney, and the White House, Milton, (more pubs!) took place in 1913, and enabled two more circular services to be worked. In October 1936, car 112 is heading south by Bransbury Road. (G.A.Tucker/T.Dethridge Coll.)

46. Car 32 and entourage open the Fratton to Milton extension on 20th July 1909 with due pomp and circumstance. (T.Dethridge Coll.)

47. From 1909 until 1913 the White House marked the terminus of the line from Fratton Bridge. Decorated for King George V's Silver Jubilee, car 7 is reversing outside this pub. The motorman expertly harpoons the points without having to leave his post, on 4th May 1935. (G.A.Tucker/T.Dethridge Coll.)

48. The final stretch of Goldsmith Avenue (named after the last squire of Milton), passes Fratton Park, home of Portsmouth Football Club. (G.A.Tucker/T.Dethridge Coll.)

49. The arches over the old Southsea Railway were demolished and Goldsmith Avenue straightened, reopening on 7th February 1925. As a tram passes on top, the new tracks can be seen in the foreground. (L.Bern Coll.)

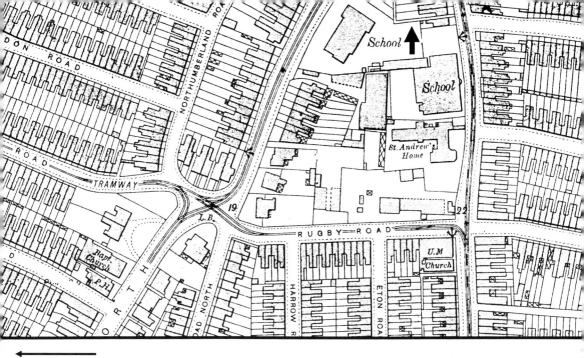

50. This was the scene by Fratton Bridge, looking east, in March 1935. Trolleybus wires for the 3/4 lead into Fawcett Road, where the tramlines were removed leaving just this triangular junction. Today a roundabout has obliterated the Fratton Electric Theatre and the Crystal Palace pub.
(G.A.Tucker/T.Dethridge Coll.)

51. Bradford Junction was always a busy interchange point. In September 1936 vestibuled car 10 is using the new trolleybus wires in Bradford Road as it prepares to turn left into Victoria Road North.
(G.A.Tucker/T.Dethridge Coll.)

52. At Somers Road there was a notorious blind corner where signalling was used from 1902 to prevent mishaps. By 1905 the property on the right-hand corner had been rebuilt to ease matters. The lowered signal arm is visible on the right. (T.Dethridge Coll.)

→

54. Car 108 traverses the same point in Somers Road which was relaid in 1933 as double track. (G.N.Southerden/J.H.Price Coll.)

53. The original interlaced tracks swept through Somers Road.
(Tramway & Railway World/J.H.Price Coll.)

→

55. Blackfriars Road leads into Greetham Street where it meets the railway. The old footbridge is about all that remains from this 1932 scene. (G.A.Tucker/T.Dethridge Coll.)

GUILDHALL - COPNOR

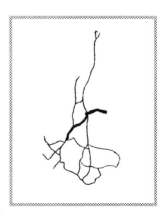

56. In 1927 the Guildhall stops were furnished with ornate iron shelters and the layout in the square was rearranged around a central loading island. Cars were boarded at the front. (C.Carter.)

57. This was the view from the Town Hall steps looking towards the Town station, circa 1910. Today both the view and the road are blocked by Council offices. (J.Welch &Sons/T.Dethridge Coll.)

58. Many early photos depict festivities when Portsmouth welcomed foreign sailors - in this case the French fleet review of August 1905, seen proceeding up Commercial Road. Fifty-nine special cars were needed, depleting regular services, and the whole fleet was dressed up for the occasion. (J.C.Bell Coll.)

59. A little further north and we are in the heart of Portsmouth's shopping district - today a pedestrian area. The French are again seen attracting the crowds, whilst a two-horse brake is stranded in Edinburgh Road.
(A.D.Packer Coll.)

8G 4382
Portsmouth Corporation Trys.

½d

South
ade Pier

Rugby
Road

Town
Hall

Dockyard

Issued subject to the Corporation Bye-laws, and available only on Car on which issued and for Section opposite punched. Must be shown to the Inspectors & given up on demand.

77

EXTRA
Section | Section | Section
1 | 2 | G

60. At the same spot, this overhead view, included for the benefit of modelmakers, caught the motorman on his blind side!
(T.Dethridge Coll.)

61. Commercial Road looking south - today nothing remains from the tramway era; the only recognisable feature is the curve in the road. (J. Welch & Sons)

62. Copnor cars turned right and proceeded up Lake Road. A horse tram passes the old Princes Theatre and Baptist church. Bombing and redevelopment have obliterated the past in this area. (T. Dethridge Coll.)

63. Having joined Kingston Road by the Tramway Arms public house, the Copnor route turned into New Road. Cosham-bound car 45 is on the Sultan Road passing loop in April 1934. Three months previously Buckland Methodist church had closed for subsequent demolition to widen Kingston Road. The notice is telling worshippers to go to the Oddfellows Hall for their service. (G.A.Tucker/T.Dethridge Coll.)

64. The tram terminus at Copnor Bridge was alongside a terrace of houses built of white-glazed bricks, overlooking Kingston Cemetery. Car 116 now has a swivel-head trolley for compatibility with the trolleybus wires. A bamboo pole is carried on the side of the tram and this was used by the crew to turn the trolley pole at termini; it was also handy in emergencies after a dewirement. The Copnor routes succumbed to trolleybuses on 1st November 1936, leaving just the Eastney routes.
(G.A.Tucker/T.Dethridge Coll.)

LANDPORT - TWYFORD AVENUE

65. This 1930s postcard illustrates the busy scene at Charlotte Street junction - Lake Road is to the right. A Southdown Leyland Titan bus is going up Commercial Road. (T.Dethridge Coll.)

66. We witness the erecting of the overhead in Commercial Road, north of Lake Road, in that busy summer of 1901. (T.Dethridge Coll.)

67. The May Day parade has passed through Mile End, followed by a parade of delayed trams! We are looking south from Sultan Road - Charles Dickens' birthplace is a little way down on the right. This is now a museum in a part of Commercial Road bypassed by the new Mile End Road. Even a short length of tramrail remains in the peaceful enclave. (T.Dethridge Coll.)

68. Car 22 passes Mile End cemetery. Except for the Market House Tavern, this area has been swept away completely. The continental ferry port car park has replaced the cemetery. (G.A.Tucker/T.Dethridge Coll.)

69. Standing outside the Air Balloon public house, Mr.Tucker photographed the junction of Kingston Crescent (right) with Twyford Avenue. Today all he would see is an elevated roundabout! (G.A.Tucker/T.Dethridge Coll.)

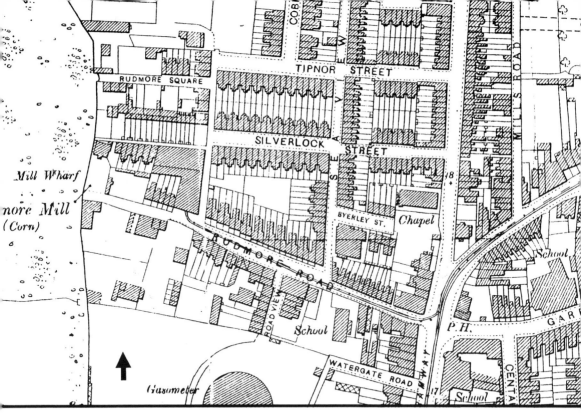

The 1898 map shows Rudmore Horsecar
depot; access was via a turntable.

70. Looking east along Kingston Crescent in
1901, a horse tram is standing under the new
wires. This busy link road is still pleasantly
tree-lined. (T.Dethridge Coll.)

71. The Twyford Avenue route was the first of three extensions built in 1913, opening on 4th July of that year.
(G.A.Tucker/T.Dethridge Coll.)

72. On a chilly spring day in 1935 we see car 36 by Alexandra Park. This was the end of the line for trams, but when trolleybuses took over in November 1935, they continued up Northern Parade to Cosham.
(G.A.Tucker/T.Dethridge Coll.)

FRATTON BRIDGE - COSHAM

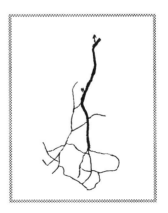

73. We now cover the long haul starting from Fratton Bridge. Circular service car 69 is about to enter one of several lengths of interlaced track which were doubled in the 1928/29 road widening scheme. In the distance is the lofty tower of St. Mary's Portsea.
(J.Welch & Sons/B.Cox Coll.)

74. This was the view from the Tramway Arms looking south along Fratton Road. Lake Road is to the right. The old pub was rebuilt when the road was widened, but the tramway as far as St. Mary's Church was abandoned in 1934. (A.D.Packer Coll.)

75. The Tramway Arms is pictured in 1927 before redevelopment took place. The south curve into Lake Road was only used by the water cars, for which a pillar hydrant was provided. Note also the tram signal above and right of car 74. This was installed in 1922 at the request of Albert Tull, the long-suffering points-boy who kept traffic moving here in all weathers. Lads recruited as points-boys worked a six day week for the princely reward of seventeen shillings and fourpence (87p)! (T.Dethridge Coll.)

76. Car 45 passes between heaven and earth, in Kingston Road. Sadly St. Stephens, Buckland parish church was bombed. The George & Dragon remains, emblazoned with the mosaic design *Brickwoods Brilliant Ales*. (G.A.Tucker/T.Dethridge Coll.)

77. Continuing along Kingston Road in its pre-widened days, car 49 approaches Queens Road. The former Majestic cinema in the distance and the terrace on the right survive - the left side was sacrificed. (G.A.Tucker/T.Dethridge Coll.)

78. At Kingston Cross a smart points-boy looks at the Edwardian photographer; two trams stand in Kingston Crescent. The busy North End shopping area starts here. (J.Welch & Sons/T.Dethridge Coll.)

79. North End shoppers are distracted by car 104, sporting its hull decorated for King George V and Queen Mary's Silver Jubilee in 1935. The slogan *Long May They Reign* did not apply to the trams! The depot was in Gladys Avenue, to the left. (B.Cox Coll.)

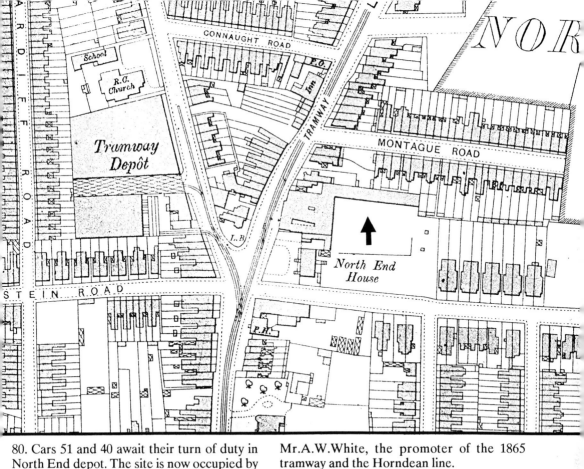

80. Cars 51 and 40 await their turn of duty in North End depot. The site is now occupied by houses - Whites Court, so named after Mr.A.W.White, the promoter of the 1865 tramway and the Horndean line. (S.Pomeroy Coll.)

81. *The Tramway & Light Railway World*
featured this view of the repair shops in 1923.
An Aladdins cave for the enthusiast, but how
many lapses of Health and Safety can you spot?
(T.Dethridge Coll.)

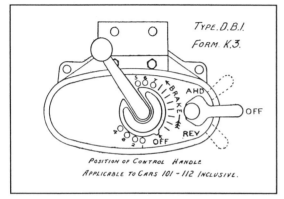

TYPE. D.B.1.
FORM. K.3.

POSITION OF CONTROL HANDLE
APPLICABLE TO CARS 101 - 112 INCLUSIVE.

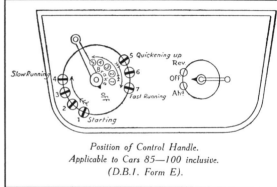

Position of Control Handle.
Applicable to Cars 85—100 inclusive.
(D.B.1. Form E).

82. A glimpse into the overhaul works in 1930
- the new number 1 is visible in undercoat. The
truck with its shaft drive and bevel gearing is
on the traverser. (T.Dethridge Coll.)

83. We head north along London Road past streets of elegant Victorian terraces with their leaded windows, iron porches and grand doorways. This is car 84, sole survivor of the tram fleet, passing a chemist's which is still trading on the corner of Hewett Road. (G.A.Tucker/T.Dethridge Coll.)

Intoxicated Persons.

34. Conductors must not allow any person in a state of intoxication, or who from any other cause is unfit to be a passenger, to board or enter their car or bus. Should any have been allowed inadvertently to do so, they shall be asked quietly to alight, and in the event of refusal, they shall be removed from the car or bus. This must be done as quietly and gently as possible, so as not to cause any confusion or alarm among the other passengers, and when available, the assistance of the Police should be obtained.

84. Moving on past the Green Posts pub - the town boundary until 1904 - we pass the old artillery barracks. This part of the 3/4 route was abandoned on 4th August 1934; car 29 is seen on 10th June of that year.
(G.A.Tucker/T.Dethridge Coll.)

85. The old Coach & Horses at Hilsea was rebuilt in 1931 - so was vestibuled car 11, bedecked with flags for the Silver Jubilee. It is seen on 11th May 1935, after regular tram services to Cosham had ceased. In 1919 work almost started on a new route from here to Copnor and Milton.
(G.A.Tucker/T.Dethridge Coll.)

86. A horsecar squeezes through Hilsea
Arches, reminding us that Portsea Island was
heavily fortified in Lord Palmerston's day. The
arches went in 1920, and today's dual
carriageway makes this a very distant memory.
Portsdown Hill looms on the horizon.
(T.Dethridge Coll.)

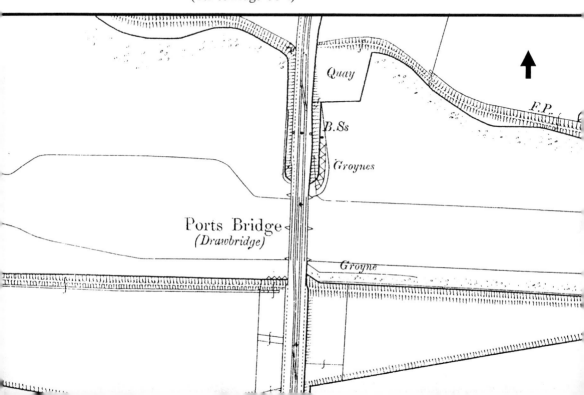

Quay

F.P.

B.Ss

Groynes

Ports Bridge
(Drawbridge)

Groyne

87. Having crossed the moat, another bridge carried the road over Ports Creek. This one replaced an older iron structure in 1927. Until 1940 this was the only road on to Portsea Island. Today this view is blocked by the M27 flyover. (S.E.Harrison)

88. A little further is the point where the new reserved track left the road, heading straight for Cosham compound. In the foreground are the disused street tracks; car 43 is seen on 20th August 1932. (G.A.Tucker/T.Dethridge Coll.)

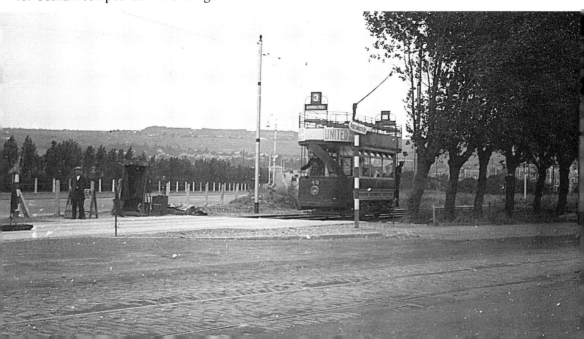

89. Another fine view at this location, looking north. Today the alignment is marked by lines of tall poplars through the sports ground. (G.A.Tucker/T.Dethridge Coll.)

90. Just north of the last two views is the point at which the Horndean line originally diverged from Portsmouth Road, by Chatsworth Avenue. This is April 1930; the reserved tracks opened in May 1932. In the centre of the photo is the old meter box used to record the power supplied by the Corporation to the Light Railway. (G.N.Southerden)

91. The original horse tram terminus at Cosham was in the middle of the road, at the level crossing gates. Later this was moved closer to the parade of shops. Crowds are seen returning from the fair on Portsdown Hill. (R.J.Harley Coll.)

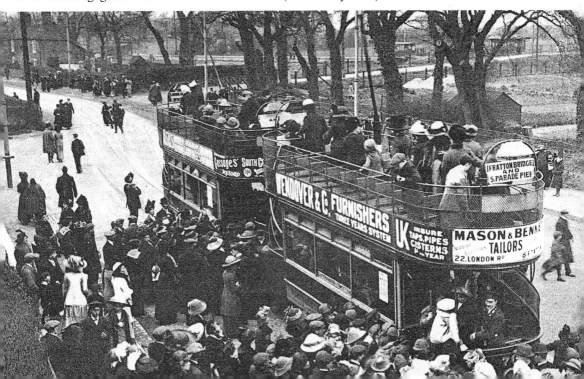

92. In 1920 Cosham compound was created - this was an off-road turning circle next to the Horndean line. It survives in smaller form with the iron shelter from Park Road. The Karrier six-wheel bus is heading for the Red Lion in the centre of Cosham. (J.H.Price Coll.)

93. This later view of the compound shows a new trolleybus on the converted route 3/4 - behind is the Light Railway's bridge over the railway. Trams last ran to Cosham on 6th October 1935. (W.J.Haynes)

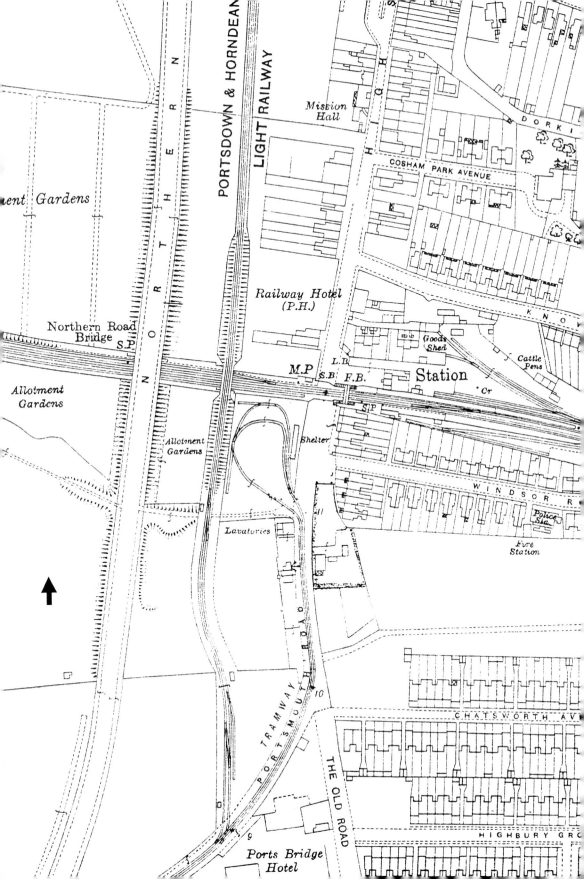

Gardens

PORTSDOWN & HORNDEAN LIGHT RAILWAY

N O R T H E R N

Mission
Hall

COSHAM PARK AVENUE

DORKI

K N O V

Railway Hotel
(P.H.)

Northern Road
Bridge **S.P**

Goods
Shed

Cattle
Pens

M.P L.B
S.B **F.B.** **Station** *Cr*

Allotment
Gardens

Allotment
Gardens

S.P

Shelter

W I N D S O R R

Police
Sta.

Lavatories

Fire
Station

TRAMWAY

PORTSMOUTH ROAD

10

C H A T S W O R T H A V

THE OLD ROAD

9

H I G H B U R Y G R O

Ports Bridge
Hotel

94. Corporation cars ran up Portsdown Hill as part of the legal settlement with the Portsdown & Horndean line, but it was not a lucrative exercise. Car 47 heads towards the hill with only the Queen Alexandra Hospital and Fort Widley in sight. Needless to say, all of this has been developed since - and is therefore in even more need of this sort of transport infrastructure! (M.Petch Coll.)

FINALE

95. By the early 1930s the contorted track layout had seriously weakened the wooden frames of the tram fleet - many creaked and leaked inside. Southdown buses provided a much higher standard of comfort. (M.J.OConnor)

96. Cosham compound on 4th August 1934 - the first day of trolleybus operation. The Crossley Condor diesel bus and tram 70 complete the line-up. (G.A.Tucker/T.Dethridge Coll.)

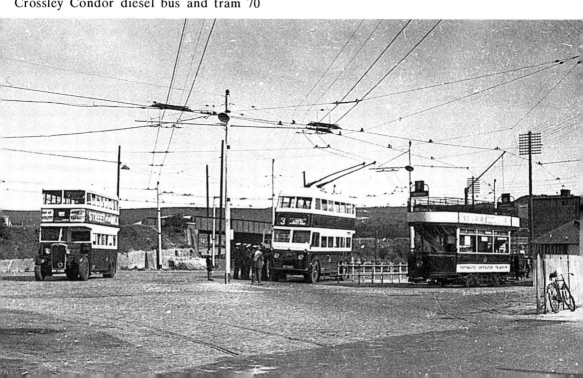

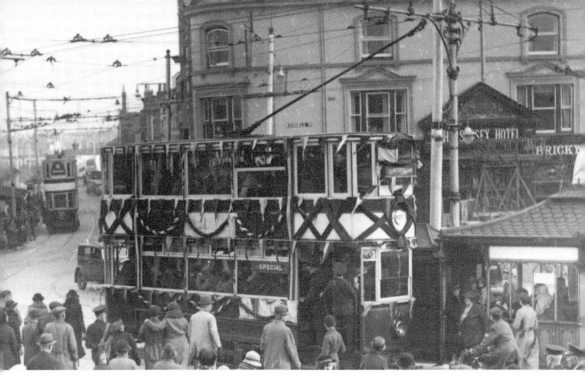

97. The last tram routes were the 5/6 and 17/18, and these finished on Tuesday 10th November 1936. Four decorated cars made the final journey to Eastney depot - car 106 leaves Guildhall Square with a very full load. (T.Dethridge Coll.)

98. It was hoped to sell the twelve enclosed cars, but as no operator showed any interest they too were broken up at Eastney. Only car 1 was sold on, to Sunderland. (T.Dethridge Coll.)

99. With some forethought, car 84 was set aside, languishing at North End then Eastney until this depot was redeveloped in 1991. It has since been in the care of Tram 57 Project in the rival city of Southampton!! In the author's opinion, this grand old lady should remain a static exhibit. (L.N.Smith)

HORSE TRAMS

100. The Evening News published this photograph in February 1933, stating that this relic was once used on the Town Station to Clarence Pier service. Another early postcard seems to confirm this.
(T.Dethridge Coll.)

101. As the system developed, so cars on each route had their own livery - yellow, green or chocolate. This is one of the cars built in 1890 by North Metropolitan Tramways for Provincial. Four of this batch were later rebuilt as electric cars. (T.Dethridge Coll.)

102. A single-deck version, of similar style to the previous view, is depicted on the service from The Hard to Lake Road, circa 1881. (T.Dethridge Coll.)

103. Cars 60 to 69 were the last Portsmouth horse trams, being built in Preston in 1894. In those far-off days, drivers earned from a guinea to twenty-seven shillings and sixpence (£1.05 to £1.37) per week; conductors had to provide their own caps! Fares were in penny stages, up to 4d(2p). (T.Dethridge Coll.)

LIFU

104. The only rail vehicle built by the Liquid Fuel Engineering Co. of East Cowes, LIFU burned paraffin to heat its boiler, which was located between the two saloons. The flue passed through a knifeboard seat on the open-sided top deck. Painted blue, it pulled one or two trailers on its route, Town Hall to North End, between 1896 and 1901. Retained by Provincial, LIFU remained as an office outside Cowplain depot until 1935. (M.Petch Coll.)

ELECTRIC CARS
1 - 80

105. The first eighty electric trams were built by Dick, Kerr of Preston to a standard design, but with reversed stairs. It was claimed that these were safer to descend while the car was moving. The six-foot/1828mm Brill truck had two 25 horse-power motors. (G.N.Southerden)

106. Ben Hall initiated a programme of car rebuilds from 1929, treating some 26 of the open-toppers. Only cars 10 and 11 received vestibules; note also the flush sides on this tram. Councillors baulked at spending £50 for upholstering car seats, yet were quite happy to leech away profits into rate relief! (G.A.Tucker/T.Dethridge Coll.)

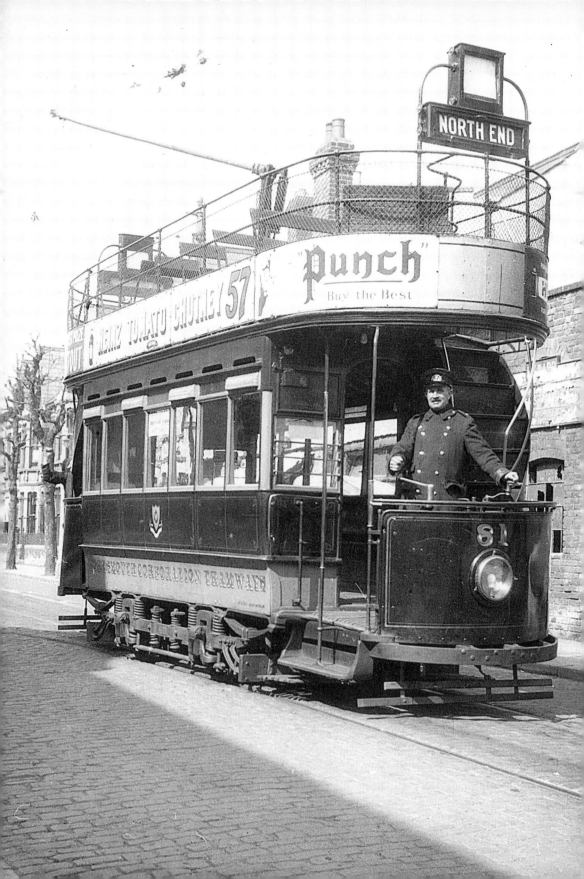

Ex-Horsecars 81 - 84

107. The Corporation decided to rebuild the best horse tram bodies as electric cars; the four involved were dealt with at North End at a cost of £470 each and entered service on 4th August 1903 - the bank holiday (see cover photo). Having no interior lights, these cars tended to be used for bank holiday and rush-hour extras. (G.N.Southerden/J.H.Price Coll.)

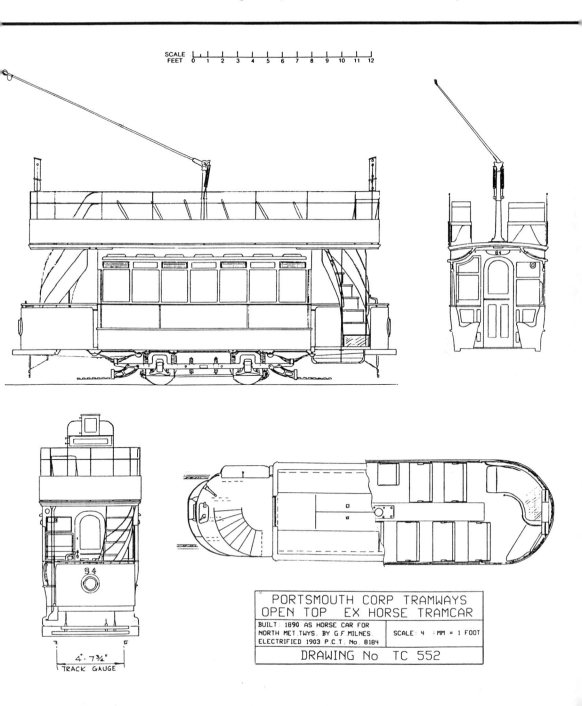

SCALE FEET 0 1 2 3 4 5 6 7 8 9 10 11 12

4'- 7¾"
TRACK GAUGE

PORTSMOUTH CORP TRAMWAYS OPEN TOP EX HORSE TRAMCAR	
BUILT: 1890 AS HORSE CAR FOR NORTH MET.TWYS. BY G.F.MILNES. ELECTRIFIED 1903 P.C.T. No. 8184	SCALE: 4 :MM = 1 FOOT
DRAWING No TC 552	

108. A further 16 cars were ordered in 1905 to cover for maintenance and for the sheer popularity of the service. Also built by Dick, Kerr, but with direct stairs at the behest of the Board of Trade, they seated 22 inside and 32 out. Notice the descriptive menu-board of destinations. (G.N.Southerden.)

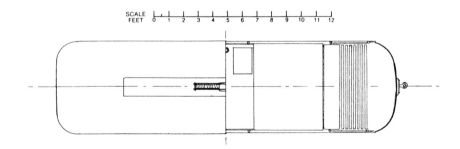

SCALE FEET 0 1 2 3 4 5 6 7 8 9 10 11 12

Water Cars 101 - 103
(101 first numbered 85)

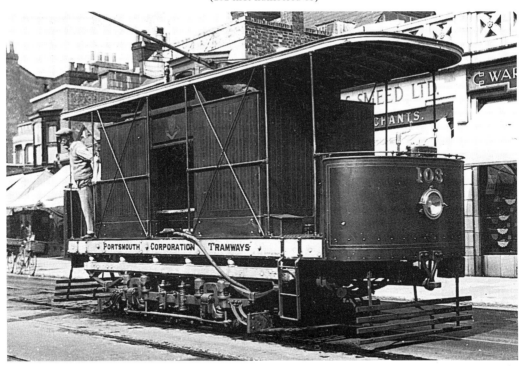

109. Water cars were used to keep down street dust, and to lubricate curves so as to reduce noise. Car 101 was built at North End in 1904 and fitted with fearsome brushes to clean out the rails. Cars 102 and 103 followed in 1919, having equipment to spray the whole road width. Car 103 was additionally a railgrinder. (G.A.Tucker/T.Dethridge Coll.)

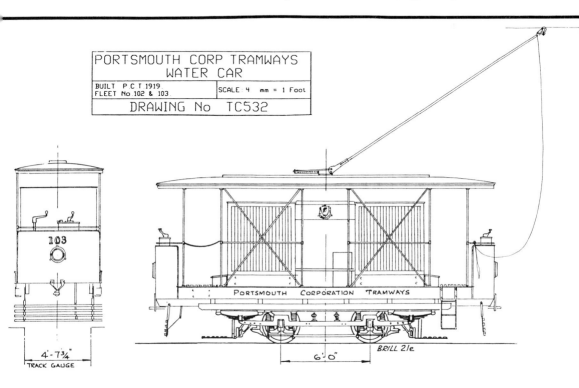

PORTSMOUTH CORP TRAMWAYS
WATER CAR

BUILT P.C.T 1919.
FLEET No 102 & 103

SCALE 4 mm = 1 Foot

DRAWING No TC532

103

PORTSMOUTH CORPORATION TRAMWAYS

4'-7¾"
TRACK GAUGE

6'0"

BRILL 21e

Toastrack Car 104

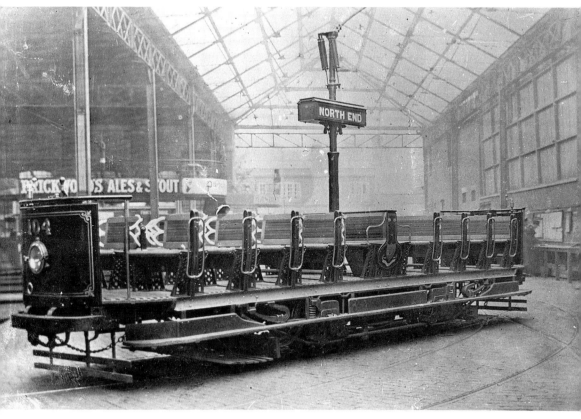

110. Built in 1914 by Southampton Corporation, this vehicle was acquired by Portsmouth in 1919 for use as a touring car. A top cover was added in 1930 when it started to be used as the illuminated car, and finally a boat-shaped body was fitted in 1933.
(Tramway Museum Society)

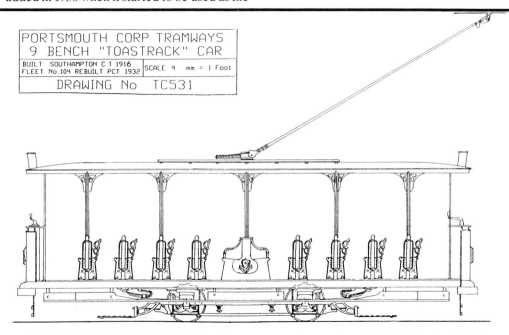

PORTSMOUTH CORP TRAMWAYS
9 BENCH "TOASTRACK" CAR

BUILT SOUTHAMPTON C T 1916
FLEET No.104 REBUILT PCT 1932

SCALE 4 mm = 1 Foot

DRAWING No TC531

Cars 105 - 116

111. These twelve cars were delivered by English Electric in 1920 and provided a much higher standard of comfort to passengers and crew. (C.T.Humpidge/J.C.Bell Coll.)

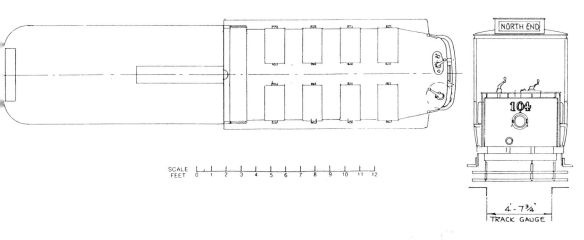

SCALE
FEET 0 1 2 3 4 5 6 7 8 9 10 11 12

NORTH END

104

4' - 7¾"
TRACK GAUGE

DRAWN BY:-TERRY RUSSELL, "CHACESIDE", ST.LEONARDS PARK, HORSHAM, W.SUSSEX. RH13 6EG.
SEND 3 FIRST CLASS STAMPS FOR COMPLETE LIST OF PUBLIC TRANSPORT DRAWINGS.

112. A detail view of the top deck shows the enclosed stairwell. This may evoke memories of thick tobacco smoke! (G.A.Tucker/T.Dethridge Coll.)

Ben Hall's Car

113. New car 1 appeared in October 1930. Equipped with a Peckham cantilever truck of 8ft./2439mm wheelbase, it had worm-drive gears and air brakes. Series production did not take place, and this fine tram was sold to Sunderland in 1936 where it ran until 1953. The original number 1 was renumbered as 53 - this car had been scrapped. (R.J.Harley Coll.)

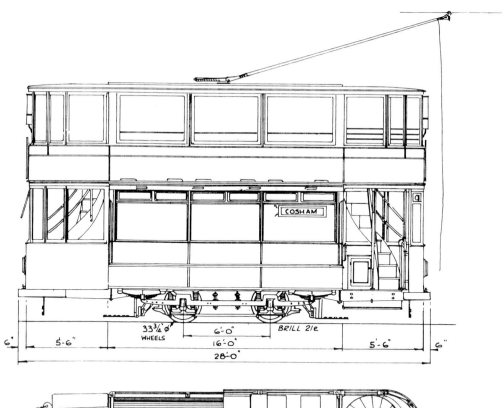

33¾" ∅ WHEELS
6'-0"
BRILL 21e
6" 5-6" 16'-0" 5-6" 6"
28'-0"
COSHAM

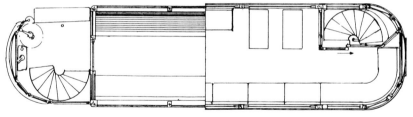

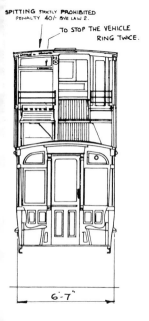

SPITTING STRICTLY PROHIBITED
PENALTY 40/- BYE LAW 2.

TO STOP THE VEHICLE
RING TWICE.

SCALE
FEET 0 1 2 3 4 5 6 7 8 9 10 11 12

6'-7"

PORTSMOUTH CORP TRAMWAYS
TOTALLY ENCLOSED CAR

BUILT ENGLISH ELECTRIC 1920 FLEET No 105 – 116	SCALE 4 mm = 1 Foot

DRAWING No TC533

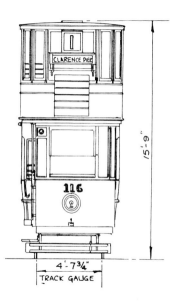

CLARENCE PIER
116
15'-9"
4'-7¾"
TRACK GAUGE

Illuminated Cars

114. Car 80 had a top cover between 1904 and 1907; it was decorated for the visit of the French Fleet in 1905. *Vive la France!* (J.Welch & Sons/J.H.Price Coll.)

115. Car 104 was latterly used as a decorated tram. Fitted with a roof, it is promoting the Lord Mayor's Joy Fund for Children. (Tramway Museum Society)

116. Car 104 in August 1933 with its recently fitted hull, is appropriately decorated for Navy Week. All of those bulbs kept the passengers warm! (D.Conrad/J.H.Price Coll.)

117. This postcard is actually a souvenir ticket, illustrating the patriotic fervour for which Portsmouth people are still renowned. (T.Dethridge Coll.)

118. This 1916 advertisement happened to feature a recent supply of tramway uniforms to Portsmouth. The dark grey serge with red edging was used right up until July 1966. (Tramway & Railway World/T.Dethridge Coll.)

119. The North End workshop staff proudly pose for the camera with car 104 - complete with a ship and the aeroplane suspended from the trolley pole. The tram is decorated for an FA Cup tie when Portsmouth met Arsenal. Unfortunately for "Pompey" fans, their team lost 2-0. The smartly overhauled trams were a tribute to these craftsmen. (B.Cox Coll.)

120. After sixty years, quite a few relics of the tramway age remain. As well as tram 84, track survives in Rugby Road, Broad Street and Old Commercial Road (above); relocated shelters can be seen in Cosham compound and Southsea Terrace. These are tangible reminders of a brief but crucial part of Portsmouth's development. (M.Petch)

POSTSCRIPT

For older residents, the Portsmouth trams are a childhood memory. It is interesting to reflect that the periods of horse and electric tram operation were roughly equal - 35 years each, while the trolleybuses sadly lasted barely 30 years.

However this is not the end of the story. Two separate projects may yet bring about the return of trams. The first is a plan for a museum line linking The Hard with Old Portsmouth via a military site earmarked for development. It is hoped that those in authority will realise the added tourist potential this would have in an already vibrant area.

Secondly, Hampshire County Council have recognised that traffic is saturating our cities, and that something radical must be done to stem this growth. Studies have shown that buses are not an incentive for motorists to change their mode of travel, and detailed planning is afoot for a Light Rail line which would link Fareham and Gosport, and proceed to Portsmouth Guildhall via a submerged tunnel. A second line could one day link Portsmouth to Waterlooville and a network may evolve, reaching Southampton and Totton. I would like to close by urging readers to give this scheme their active support so that the citizens of Portsmouth can enjoy once more a quality transport system.

MP Middleton Press

Easebourne Lane, Midhurst. West Sussex. GU29 9AZ   Tel: 01730 813169   Fax: 01730 812601
. . . . . Write or telephone for our latest list . . . . .

BRANCH LINES
Branch Line to Allhallows
Branch Lines to Alton
Branch Lines around Ascot
Branch Line to Bude
Branch Lines around Canterbury
Branch Lines to East Grinstead
Branch Lines around Effingham Jn
Branch Lines to Exmouth
Branch Line to Fairford
Branch Line to Hawkhurst
Branch Lines to Horsham
Branch Lines around Huntingdon
Branch Lines to Ilfracombe
Branch Line to Lyme Regis
Branch Line to Lynton
Branch Lines around March
Branch Lines around Midhurst
Branch Lines to Newport
Branch Line to Padstow
Branch Lines around Portmadoc 1923-46
Branch Lines around Porthmadog 1954-94
Branch Lines to Seaton & Sidmouth
Branch Line to Selsey
Branch Lines around Sheerness
Branch Line to Southwold
Branch Line to Swanage
Branch Line to Tenterden
Branch Lines to Torrington
Branch Lines to Tunbridge Wells
Branch Line to Upwell
Branch Lines around Weymouth

LONDON SUBURBAN RAILWAYS
Caterham and Tattenham Corner
Clapham Jn. to Beckenham Jn.
Crystal Palace and Catford Loop
Holborn Viaduct to Lewisham
London Bridge to Addiscombe
Mitcham Junction Lines
South London Line
West Croydon to Epsom
Willesden Junction to Richmond
Wimbledon to Epsom

STEAMING THROUGH
Steaming through Cornwall
Steaming through East Sussex
Steaming through the Isle of Wight
Steaming through Surrey
Steaming through West Hants
Steaming through West Sussex

GREAT RAILWAY ERAS
Ashford from Steam to Eurostar
Festiniog in the Fifties

COUNTRY BOOKS
Brickmaking in Sussex
East Grinstead Then and Now

SOUTH COAST RAILWAYS
Ashford to Dover
Bournemouth to Weymouth
Brighton to Eastbourne
Brighton to Worthing
Chichester to Portsmouth
Dover to Ramsgate
Hastings to Ashford
Ryde to Ventnor
Worthing to Chichester

SOUTHERN MAIN LINES
Bromley South to Rochester
Charing Cross to Orpington
Crawley to Littlehampton
Dartford to Sittingbourne
East Croydon to Three Bridges
Epsom to Horsham
Exeter to Barnstaple
Exeter to Tavistock
Faversham to Dover
Haywards Heath to Seaford
London Bridge to East Croydon
Orpington to Tonbridge
Sittingbourne to Ramsgate
Swanley to Ashford
Three Bridges to Brighton
Tonbridge to Hastings
Victoria to Bromley South
Waterloo to Windsor
Woking to Southampton
Yeovil to Exeter

COUNTRY RAILWAY ROUTES
Andover to Southampton
Bath to Evercreech Junction
Bournemouth to Evercreech Jn
Burnham to Evercreech Junction
Croydon to East Grinstead
East Kent Light Railway
Fareham to Salisbury
Guildford to Redhill
Porthmadog to Blaenau
Reading to Basingstoke
Reading to Guildford
Redhill to Ashford
Salisbury to Westbury
Strood to Paddock Wood
Taunton to Barnstaple
Westbury to Bath
Woking to Alton

TROLLEYBUS CLASSICS
Croydon's Trolleybuses
Woolwich & Dartford Trolleybuses

TRAMWAY CLASSICS
Aldgate & Stepney Tramways
Bournemouth & Poole Tramways
Brighton's Tramways
Bristol's Tramways
Camberwell & W. Norwood Tramway
Croydon's Tramways
Dover's Tramways
East Ham & West Ham Tramways
Embankment & Waterloo Tramways
Exeter & Taunton Tramways
Greenwich & Dartford Tramways
Hampstead & Highgate Tramways
Hastings Tramways
Ilford & Barking Tramways
Kingston & Wimbledon Tramways
Lewisham & Catford Tramways
Maidstone & Chatham Tramways
North Kent Tramways
Portsmouth's Tramways
Southampton Tramways
Southend-on-sea Tramways
Thanet's Tramways
Victoria & Lambeth Tramways
Walthamstow & Leyton Tramways
Wandsworth & Battersea Tramways

OTHER RAILWAY BOOKS
Garraway Father & Son
Industrial Railways of the South East
London Chatham & Dover Railway
South Eastern Railway
War on the Line

MILITARY BOOKS
Battle over Portsmouth
Battle Over Sussex 1940
Blitz Over Sussex 1941-42
Bognor at War
Bombers over Sussex 1943-45
Military Defence of West Sussex

WATERWAY ALBUMS
Hampshire Waterways
Kent and East Sussex Waterways
London to Portsmouth Waterway
West Sussex Waterways

BUS BOOK
Eastbourne Bus Story

SOUTHERN RAILWAY ● VIDEOS ●
Memories of the Hayling Island Branch
Memories of the Lyme Regis Branch
War on the Line